The m&m's® BRAND Count to One Hundred Book

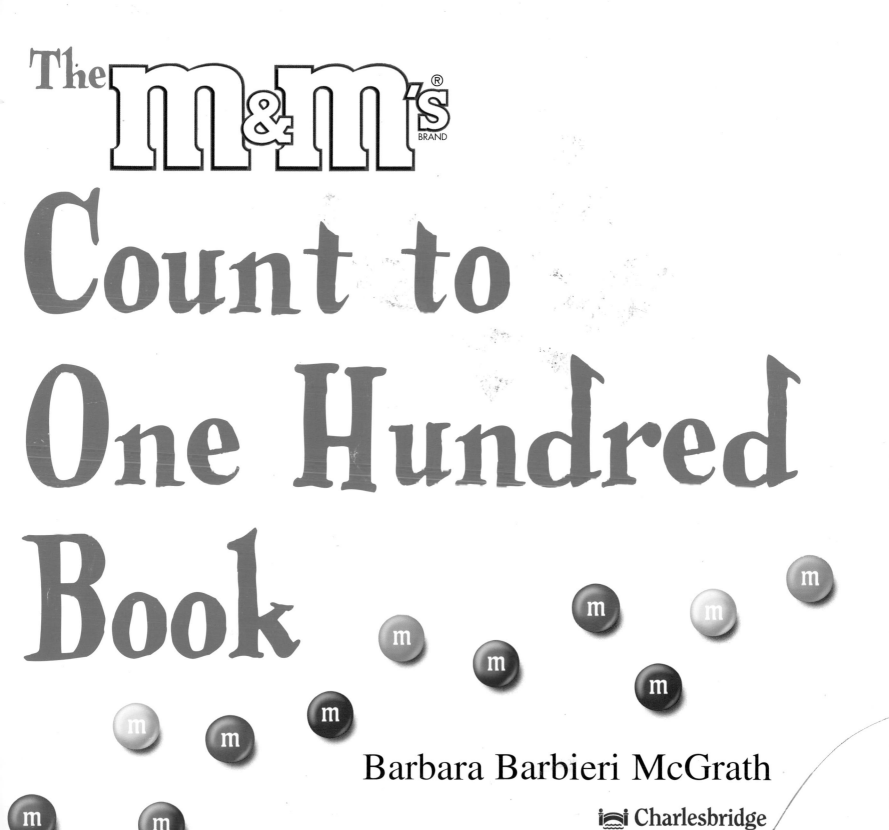

Barbara Barbieri McGrath

Charlesbridge

With M&M'S® candies we'll learn something new.
We'll count to one hundred—it's easy to do!

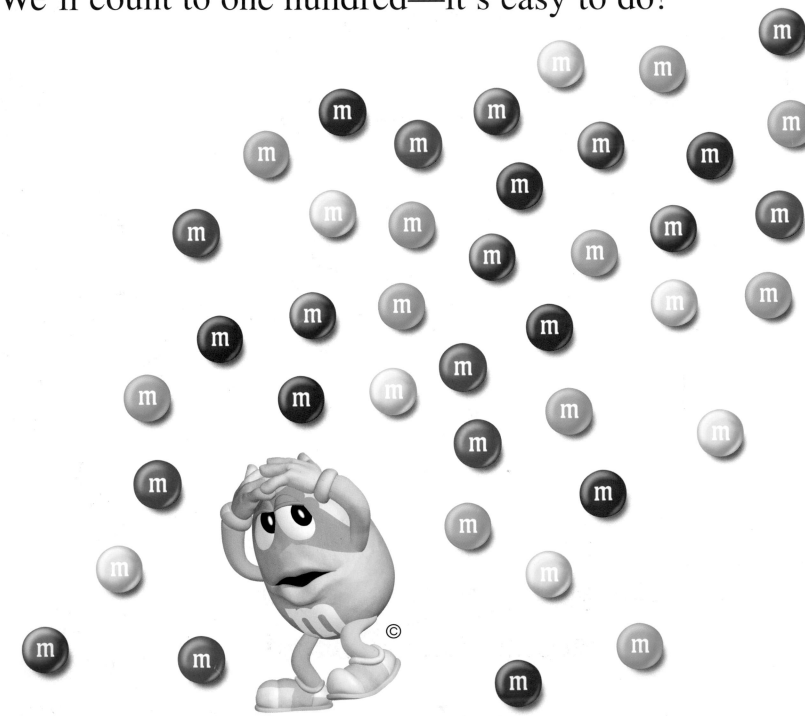

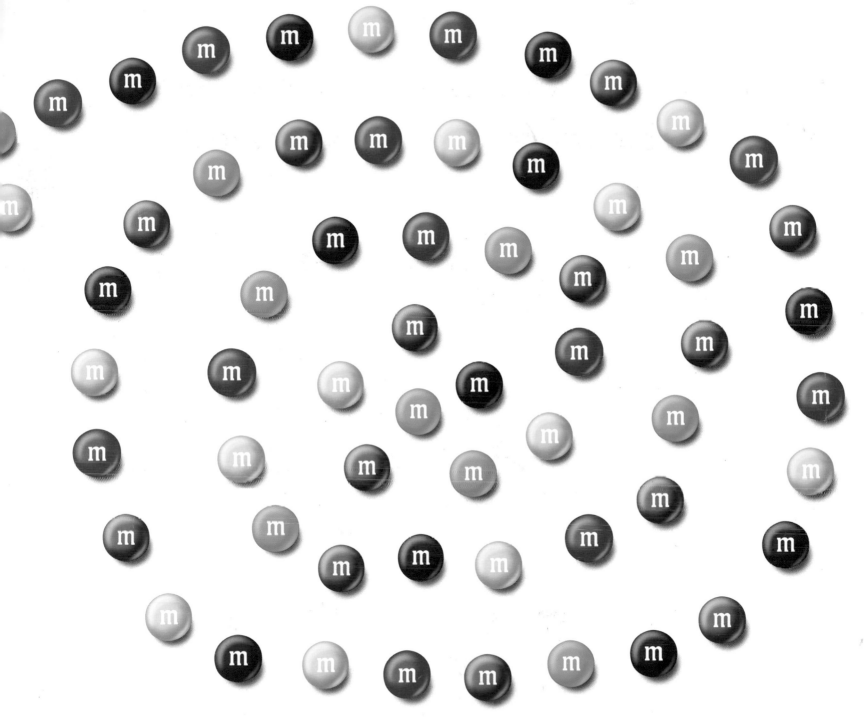

Can you think of a sweeter way
To celebrate One Hundred Day?

Before you learn something new,
It's a good idea to do a review.

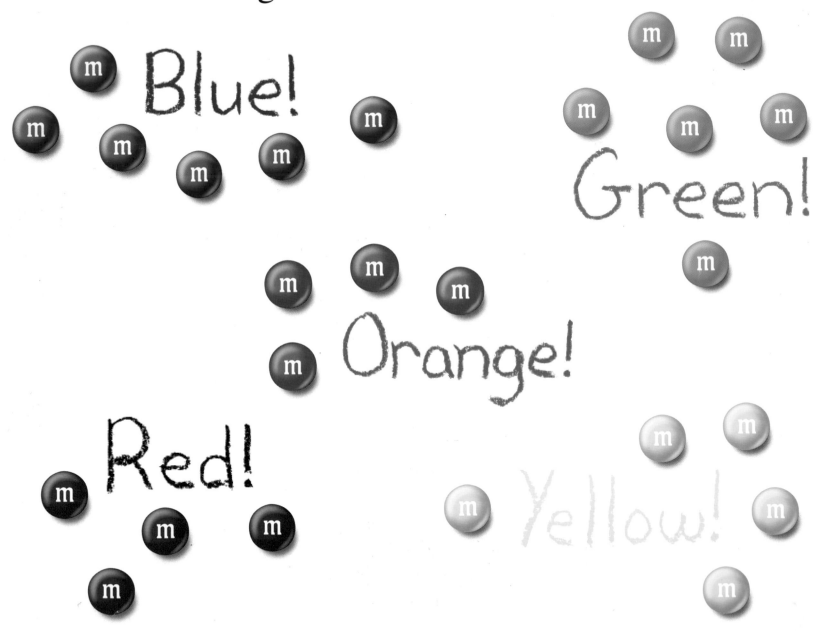

Blue!

Green!

Orange!

Red!

Yellow!

Five different colors are easy to find.

Count out ten red to warm up your mind.

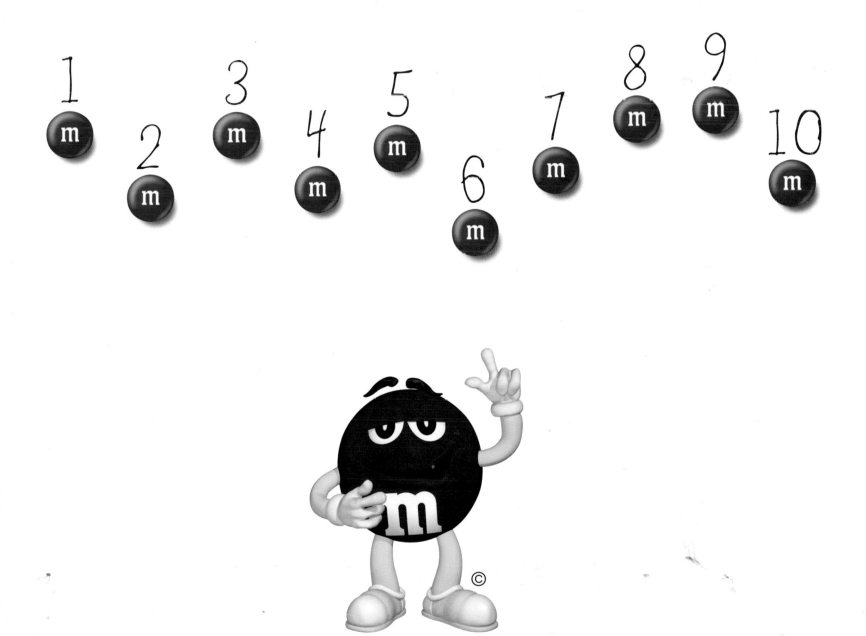

Keep counting with red.
Of those there are plenty.
Start with eleven and
Count up to twenty.

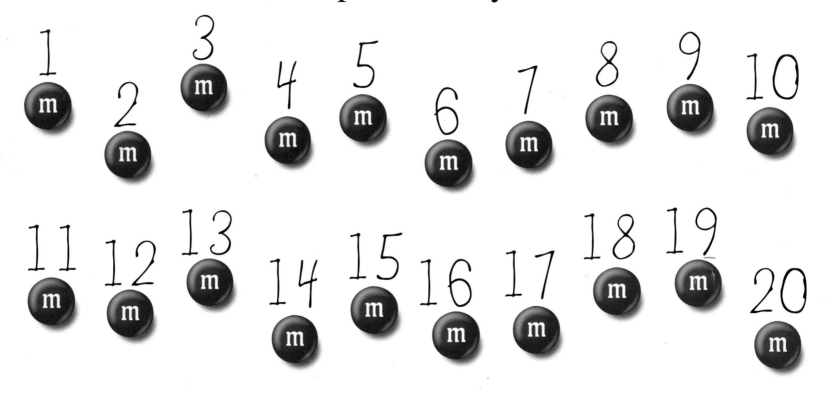

Great job! Are you ready
To count real high?
It will be fun if you give it a try.

To start, please sort
The bright color green.
Find one, then go on
Until twenty are seen.

Count out twenty green,
Yellow, orange, and blue.
Twenty of five colors
Are in front of you!

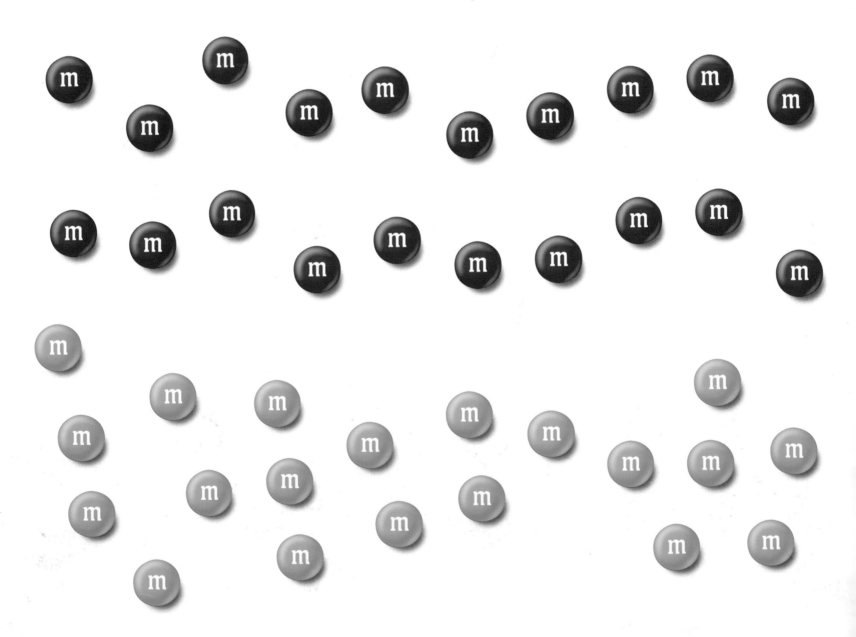

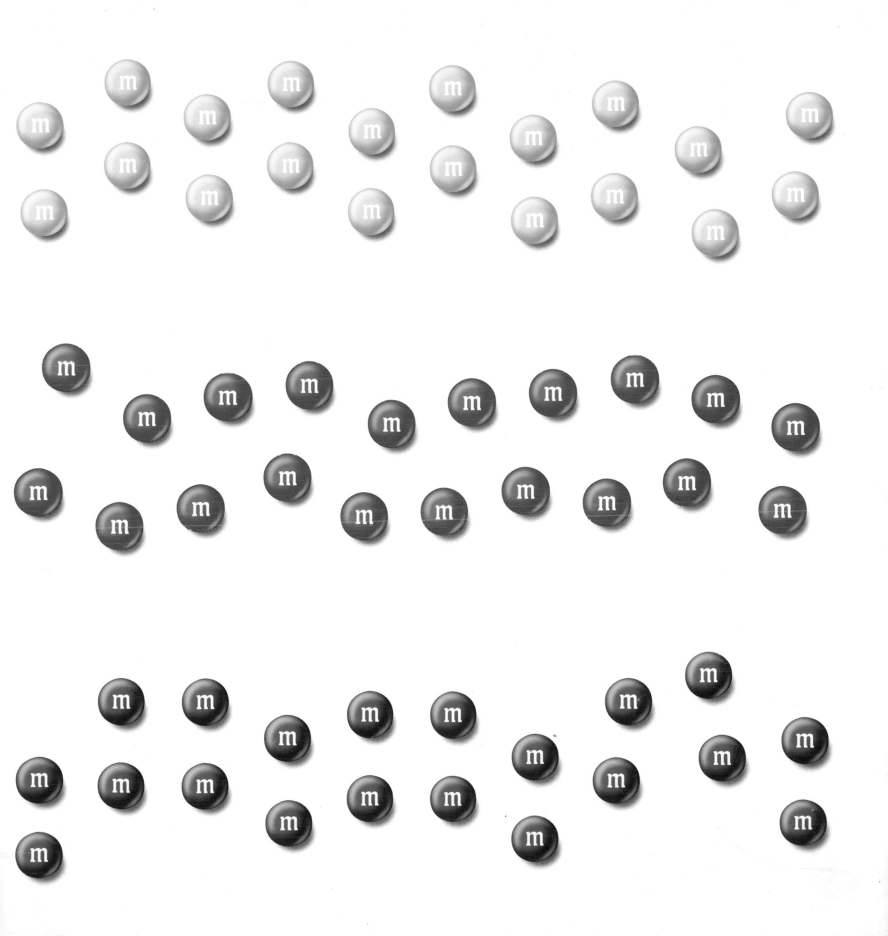

Line them up
By color ten across, then. . .
You will see five colors
In two lines of ten.

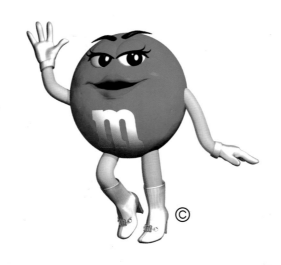

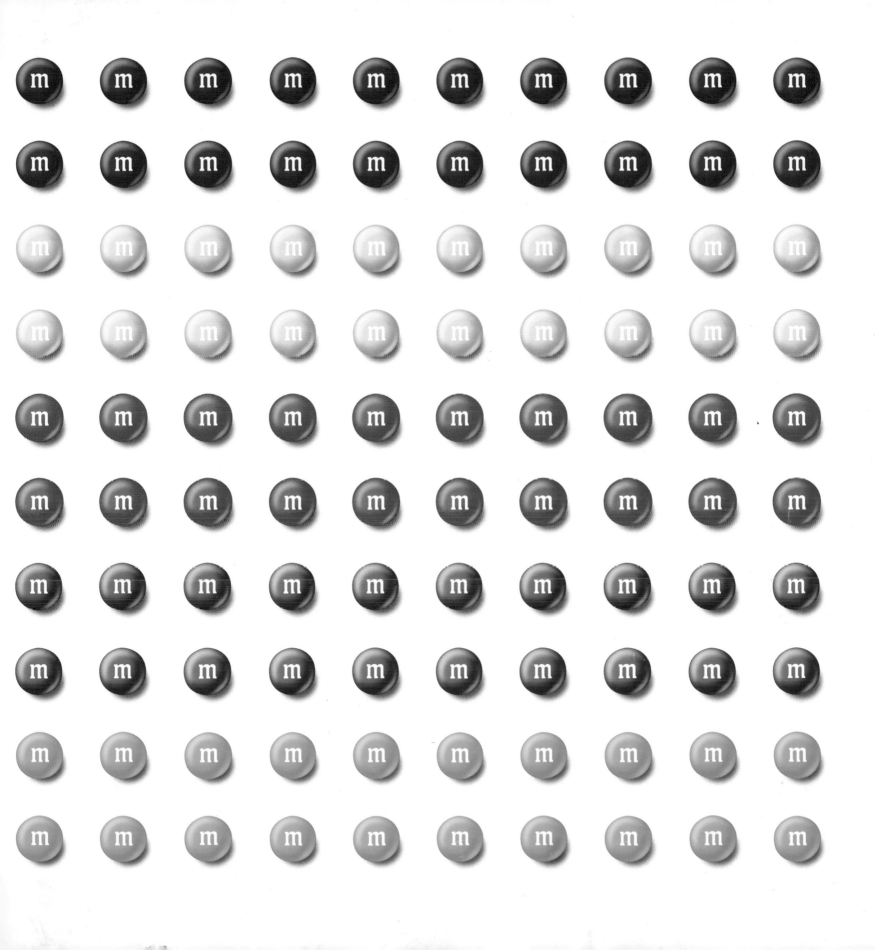

This might take a while,
So get ready, get set.
The rule is, no saying,
"Am I done yet?"

Start at the top.
Touch each one—it's a game!
Give each M&M'S® candy
Its own number name.

1	2	3	4	5	6	7	8	9	10
11	12	13	14	15	16	17	18	19	20
21	22	23	24	25	26	27	28	29	30
31	32	33	34	35	36	37	38	39	40
41	42	43	44	45	46	47	48	49	50
51	52	53	54	55	56	57	58	59	60
61	62	63	64	65	66	67	68	69	70
71	72	73	74	75	76	77	78	79	80
81	82	83	84	85	86	87	88	89	90
91	92	93	94	95	96	97	98	99	100

You counted to one hundred!
Good for you.
Take a deep breath,
Because we aren't through.

Of counting to one hundred
You are a master.
Let's learn a way
To get there much faster.

Let's skip count by tens.
So get ready to go:
Skip all the numbers
Except the last in each row.

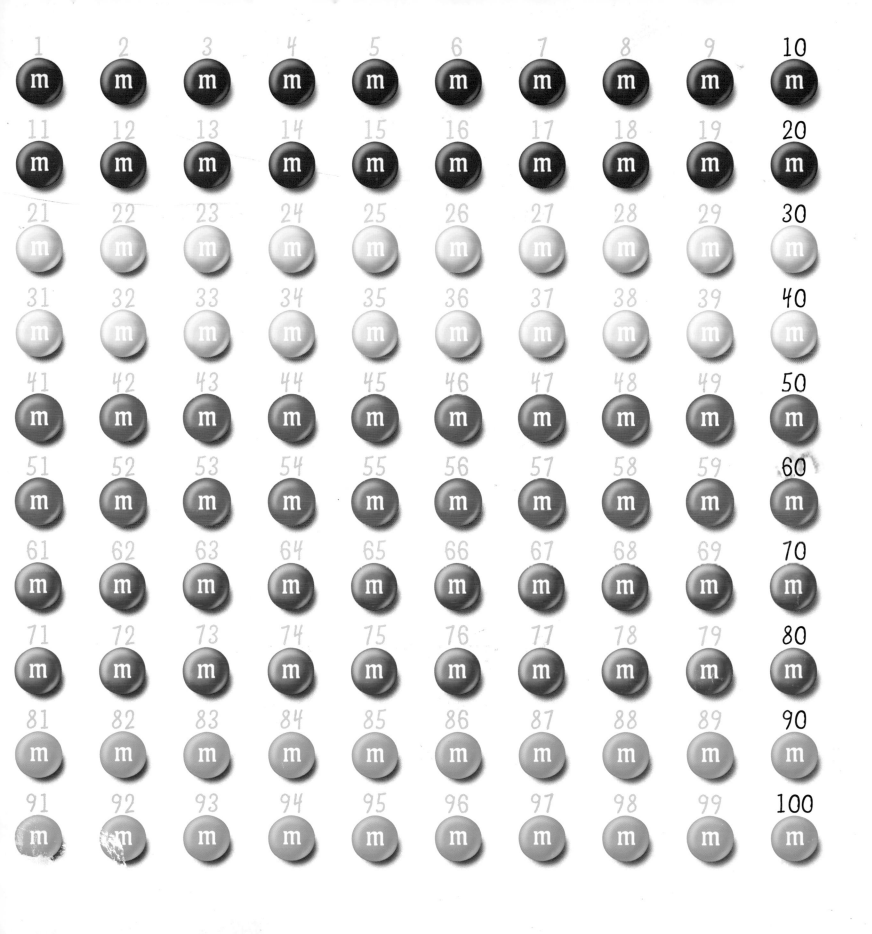

That was real quick!

Now what would you say

If we learned how

To skip count another way?

Move five candies.

It was easy—they slid!

Now make each row

Look like the one you just did.

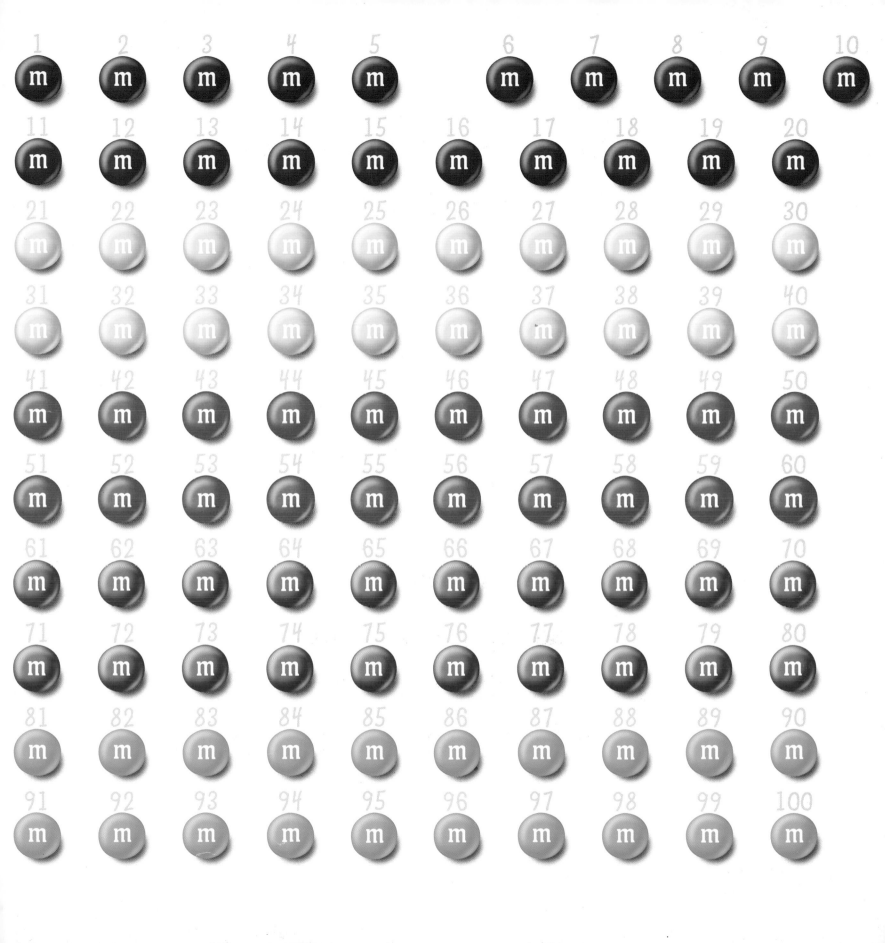

Let's skip count by fives.
Use M&M'S® as a tool.
Say the last number in each line,
That is the rule.

You did it again!
Now come on—let's see
One more way to one hundred.
Just follow me.

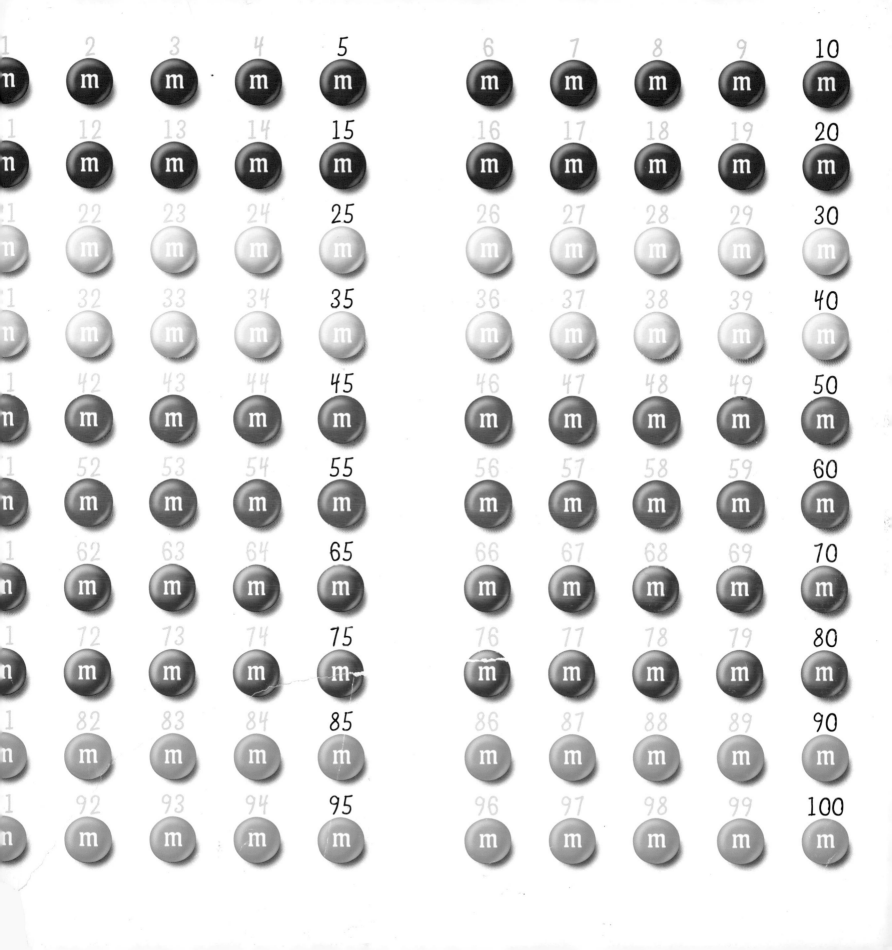

Push two M&M'S® together,
Keeping them in their line.
This might take a while;
You're doing just fine.

Two, four, six, eight, ten—
Skip counting by two
All the way to one hundred
Is a hard thing to do.

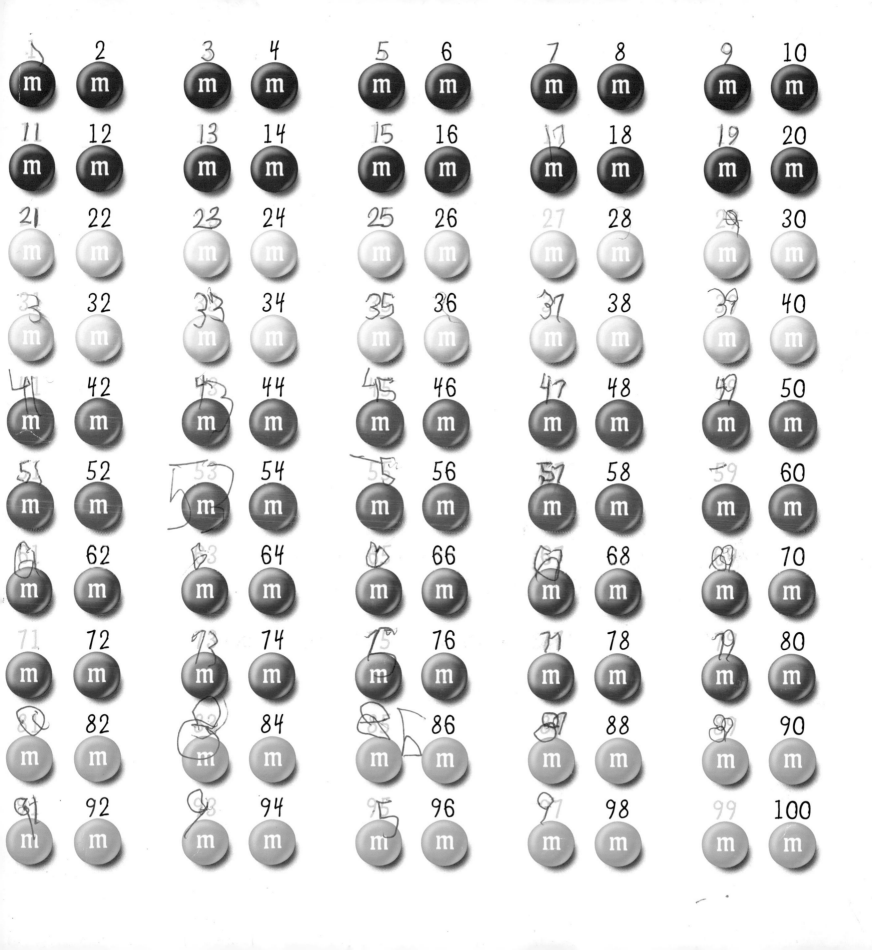

You reached one hundred
By ones, tens, fives, and twos!
When you do it again,
Which way will you choose?

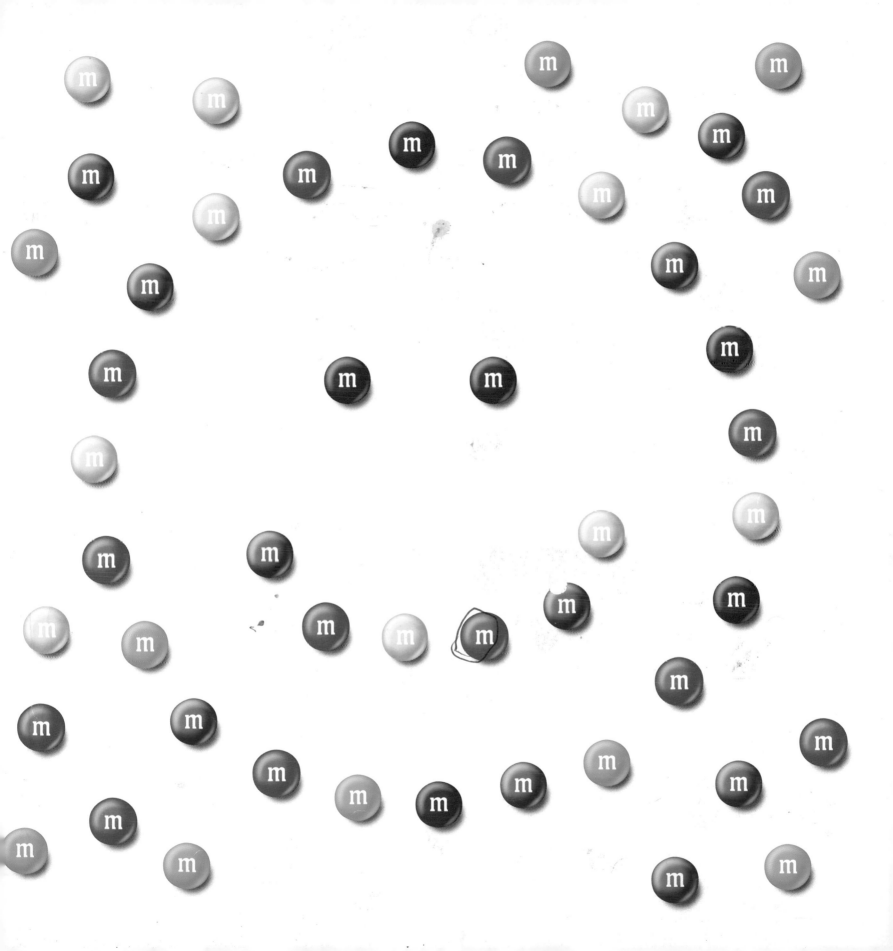

Review

Count by ones

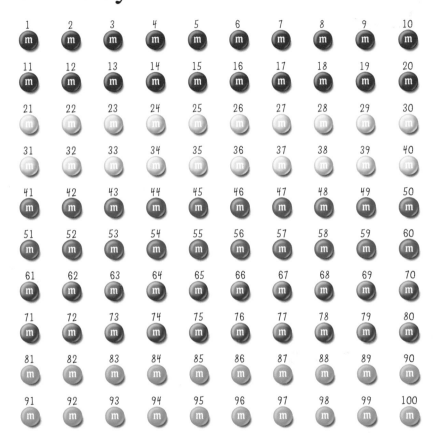

Skip count by fives

Skip count by twos

Skip count by tens

Love to Sue and Dawn

Special thanks to Dominic B., Susan S., and Randi R.

Published by Charlesbridge
85 Main Street
Watertown, MA 02472
(617) 926-0329
www.charlesbridge.com

Library of Congress Cataloging-in-Publication Data
McGrath, Barbara Barbieri, 1954-
  The M&M'S® brand count to one hundred book / Barbara Barbieri
McGrath.
      p. cm.
Summary: Explains how to count up to 100 pieces of M&M'S® candy by ones,
twos, fives, and tens.
   ISBN 1-57091-570-9 (reinforced for library use) -- ISBN 1-57091-571-7 (softcover)
   1. Counting - Juvenile literature. [1. Counting.] I. Title: M&M'S®
brand count to one hundred book. II. Title.
   QA113 .M393688 2003
   513.2'11 dc21   2002014590

Printed in South Korea

(hc) 10 9 8 7 6 5 4 3 2 1
(sc) 10 9 8 7 6 5 4 3 2 1

Display type set in Woodrow, designed by Chank Fonts; text type is Adobe Times
Printed and bound by Sung In Printing, South Korea
Production supervision by Brian G. Walker
Designed by Susan Mallory Sherman